Research Monograph Number 1

The Distribution of

Personal Wealth in Scotland

ALAN HARRISON

Lecturer in Economics, University of Strathclyde

The Fraser of Allander Institute for Research on the Scottish Economy at the University of Strathclyde

ISBN 0 904865 00 2

I. Introduction

In the foreword to the recent Green Paper on the proposed annual wealth tax [12] the Chancellor of the Exchequer states that the government "is committed to use the taxation system to promote greater economic and social equality" by effecting a redistribution of wealth. He justifies this by arguing that "the bulk of privately owned wealth is still concentrated in relatively few hands". This assertion raises two related questions, both of which have been extensively discussed in recent months. In the first place, how unequally distributed is personal wealth; and second, is the degree of inequality excessive? The latter question is clearly a matter for value judgements and as such will be considered only in the conclusion. The former question however, while affording opportunities for dispute because of the deficiencies of the basic data sources, is something about which we should be relatively sure; indeed without some firm knowledge of the degree of inequality, it is impossible to begin discussing the case for redistribution.

In this paper we attempt to provide some indication of the distribution of wealth in Scotland, comparing its concentration with that observed in England and Wales. We begin by discussing the alternative methods by which estimates of the distribution of wealth can be derived. Next we explain more fully the particular method chosen, and investigate the implications of its acknowledged limitations for the accuracy of the estimates. We then present a consistent series for the distribution in Scotland covering the years 1938 to 1969, and compare this with corresponding figures for England and Wales. Finally we discuss what light is thrown on the debate about the need for a wealth tax by the evidence we present, and offer some tentative explanations of the trends in the estimated figures.[1]

II. Estimating the Distribution of Wealth

There are three main methods by which information can be derived about the distribution of personal wealth; sample surveys, the

---

1. This paper is based on work being carried out jointly with Tony Atkinson (with the support of the Social Science Research Council) and which will be reported at greater length in a forthcoming monograph [5]. I am grateful to Tony Atkinson, Keith Ingham, David Simpson and Alan Tait for their comments on an earlier draft.

investment income method and the estate duty method. In this paper we rely on the estate duty method, a choice which it is clearly necessary to justify. This we briefly do by outlining each of the other two methods and their particular deficiencies. Section III then considers the estate duty method.

An annual sample survey providing accurate estimates of wealth-holdings for a representative sample of families or individuals would be an ideal source for the study of the personal distribution of wealth. Unfortunately there have been very few surveys and those which have been made suffer from serious shortcomings. In particular cross-checks with independent information suggest that the wealthy are under-represented, in addition to which there appears to have been significant under-statement of wealth by those taking part. In the case of the Oxford savings survey for example, Lydall and Tipping, who made use of the survey, note that "there was a response rate of only 67 per cent amongst the income units approached for interviews" and "almost certainly a substantial amount of under-statement of assets even by those who were 'successfully' interviewed" ([7], p.85). Thus it seems that at best sample surveys can only be expected to supplement our knowledge of wealth-holdings at the lower end of the distribution and this is in fact the purpose for which Lydall and Tipping used the Oxford data.

The investment income method involves capitalisation of tax data relating to investment incomes to yield an estimate of the wealth distribution. The essence of the method is to apply a "yield multiplier" to work back from the distribution of investment income to the distribution of wealth: if for example the yield is thought to be 5 per cent, the multiplier is 20 so an investment income of £5,000 is assumed to correspond to wealth of £100,000. In a recent paper [3] we have used this method to derive estimates of the distribution in Britain in 1968 and comparisons are made with the distribution implied by the estate duty method, the method we propose to use here. Our conclusion that "the investment income method is unlikely to replace the estate duty method . . . in view of the fact that the investment data have even more limited coverage than the estate data and that the results are very sensitive to the assumptions made about the yield" ([3], p.139) suggests that the most we can expect the investment income method to achieve is an external check on a certain part of the wealth distribution.

For these reasons we have therefore preferred to use the estate duty method to derive our estimates of the distribution of wealth in Scotland. This should not be taken to imply, however, that this method does not also have its shortcomings. Indeed it has been

4

argued that official estimates of the distribution of wealth in Britain based on the estate duty method[2] are grossly misleading, and that estimates should be derived using sample survey techniques ([9], p.77). We do not share this opinion, and explain our justification for this statement in the next section.

III. The Estate Duty Method

Until the wealth tax is introduced it remains the case that the only occasion when a person has to reveal his total assets and liabilities is when he dies. The returns of wealth made for the purpose of the estate duty are, therefore, an important source of information about the distribution of wealth: in effect they allow us to use the dead as a sample of living. The basic method of estimation is very straight-forward. The Inland Revenue annually publishes details of estates classified by size and by the age and sex of the deceased.[3] If it is then assumed that those of a particular age and sex dying in that year were representative of the living population, the overall distribution may be obtained by "blowing up" the estate data by a mortality multiplier equal to the reciprocal of the mortality rate. Thus if for a particular age/sex group the mortality rate is 1 in 1,000, we assume that for every person dying in this group there were 999 alive in similar circumstances and we multiply the numbers and values of estates by 1,000.

As we have noted already there are many problems associated with this method which have prompted Polanyi and Wood to argue that "the wealth of the dead . . . cannot be transformed by statistical devices to indicate the wealth of the living" ([9] back cover). It is clearly impossible in a paper of this length to consider the quantitative importance of each of the deficiencies in detail. We therefore propose to confine ourselves to some of the more important points raised by Polanyi and Wood in an attempt to assess the validity of their statement quoted above. The problems we have chosen for

2. See for example [6], table 104, p.128.

3. Until 1962 the figures were published separately for England and Wales, and Scotland and it is of course the latter we make use of here. For years after 1962 we are grateful to the Inland Revenue for making available unpublished statistics relating to Scotland. They are of course not responsible in any way for the use to which the data have been put.

discussion can be categorised under four headings: missing people, missing wealth, valuation and mortality multipliers.

The estate duty statistics cover only those estates on which duty was paid or for which grants of representation (grants of confirmation in Scotland) were issued. This presents an important problem since over half of all estates do not come to the notice of the estate duty office and are therefore excluded from the wealth estimates produced by the application of mortality multipliers. Since duty is not paid on omitted estates it seems reasonable to suppose that the majority of the people excluded are likely to own only small amounts of wealth and thus belong to the lowest ranges of estates. The usual procedure adopted therefore is to calculate the number of excluded people using a control total for the adult population and add this to the estimated number in the bottom range of the wealth distribution.[4] This, however, implicitly assumes zero wealth for all those excluded, which is clearly unsatisfactory, and in our work an estimate is made for the wealth these people are likely to be holding.

The question of what level of wealth to allocate to the excluded population is a more difficult one to answer. Polanyi and Wood for example suggest that (for 1970) "omitted estates might have been worth up to £5,000" ([9], p.39), the level of the estate duty exemption at that time. This is of course possible although it is extremely unlikely that the *average* figure was equal to £5,000.[5] Alternative methods of deriving a more precise figure are available, such as the use of sample survey data and national balance sheet data, and this is the technique we adopt to adjust our estimates of the distribution of wealth.[6]

Besides the wealth which is missing from the estate duty statistics because of omitted estates, there is also a substantial amount which escapes duty, and hence the statistics, because of provisions in the estate duty law which allow wealth to be transferred without duty being paid. Probably the most important item in this category is settled property;[7] Revell [10] estimated the total missing in 1961 on

---

4. For example the Inland Revenue make alternative estimates of the degree of inequality which are based on this procedure ([6], p.176).

5. For the same year estates below the exemption level averaged less than £1,900, and independent information suggests this to be substantially in excess of the average for excluded persons.

6. For the details see the appendix to Atkinson [2].

7. For example, property settled on a surviving spouse (with no power to dispose of the capital) is exempt on the death of the spouse.

this account to be £1,600 million which is to be compared with £55,000 million total wealth estimated by the Inland Revenue from the estate duty statistics. It is widely acknowledged that this exclusion suggests an artificially low degree of inequality since these items are likely to be held disproportionately by the wealthy. Significantly Polanyi and Wood neglect to consider this point in detail, or other missing wealth such as that held overseas, and for this reason their conclusion that "the major bias . . . seems to be towards the under-statement . . . of those types of wealth which are particularly widely spread among the majority" ([9], p.31) is not necessarily justified.

Another major exclusion which perhaps fits the above description more closely is that of pension rights and other assets which disappear on death. However whether or not this necessitates an adjustment depends on the method of valuation. This question was discussed in some detail by Revell [10] and he concluded that "in general the valuation of items for estate duty is just what we need - a valuation at market prices". However it is not quite as straight-forward as he indicates since market value may be an ambiguous concept, so that a number of different definitions could be adopted. This point is of crucial importance in the context of the current debate about the degree of inequality which characterises the distribution of wealth and we therefore feel the need to consider it in some detail.

In previous work we have distinguished between the value obtainable on realisation ("sell-up" value) and the value to a person or household as a "going concern". The Inland Revenue valuation, mentioned by Revell, is closer to the former. In the case of household goods for example, the valuation is based on second-hand prices which (with certain exceptions, e.g. cars) are clearly lower than the value as a going concern. Similarly pension rights (from both state and private sources) in general have no "sell-up" value,[8] although they do have a value as a going concern. Thus Polanyi and Wood, who argue for an adjustment for these deficiencies, seem implicitly to make the assumption that the going concern is the appropriate method of valuation. It is however imperative that the definition chosen should be consistently applied to all assets and liabilities, and here again Polanyi and Wood can be criticised. They fail to take account of the fact that certain assets which are predominately to be found higher up the wealth distribution, such as trade assets of

---

8.   The holder typically cannot for example realise his pension rights or use them as
     security for a loan.

unincorporated businesses, will also increase in value if a going concern basis is applied. Thus once again it seems that their choice of examples has been tailored to fit the point they are trying to make.

The distinction we are making can be seen then as the difference between the realisation value of an asset and its value to the individual if he retains it. The problems this presents can be further illustrated by the example of life policies. For estate duty purposes these are valued at the sum assured (plus bonuses), which is at variance with the Inland Revenue method generally applied, that of a 'sell-up' basis. This is because the realisation value of a policy, while being positive, is only the surrender value, which is always less than the sum assured. On the other hand the surrender value is clearly not appropriate for a going concern, because of the penalty which such a value is intended to impose.

Perhaps a prior question to that of valuation is the definition of wealth adopted. An asset where this is important is the property right associated with a council house tenancy and indeed Polanyi and Wood advocate that estimates of the distribution of wealth should include an adjustment for public housing. They further argue that this inclusion would have a significant downward effect on the degree of inequality. In our estimates we make no such allowance. However it is essential that this is made explicit, especially since publicly-provided housing forms a very high proportion of the total housing stock in Scotland. Thus its effect on the distribution if it were included, would probably be greater than the effect of an equivalent adjustment for England and Wales. However it must also be noted that the "ownership" of council house property rights in Scotland is generally acknowledged to reach further up the wealth scale than in England and Wales which, if true, may partially offset the equalising effect.

There is of course no "correct" definition or method of valuation and the choice will depend on the use to which the estimates will be put. A further consideration is the adequacy of data which is perhaps a more important constraint in our case. In this paper we have therefore opted for a 'sell-up' basis essentially by accepting the Inland Revenue valuation, and have extended this when making estimates of the wealth of the excluded population, although we have made no allowances for other forms of missing wealth. It must be emphasised that this leaves at least two unresolved problems. As we noted earlier life policies are over-stated since the sum assured is the figure used in estate duty statistics. On the other hand the existence of settled property is ignored. The most we can say at the present time about the effects of these is that the latter will understate the degree of inequality, but it is impossible without further research to state the direction of bias of the former factor.

The final problem concerned with the estate duty method is that of the appropriate mortality multipliers to use. As we have noted already the total number and value of estates in each cell is multiplied by the relevant multiplier (the reciprocal of the mortality rate). The cells are classified by age and sex to allow for differing mortality experience, and a further classification by estate size is made so that the multipliers can be adjusted for variations in mortality with economic status. This is usually done by assuming that wealth is correlated with social class and applying social class differentials to the multipliers for estates above a certain size. For example, if the differential is 0.8 (mortality in social classes I and II, those usually used, is 80 per cent of overall mortality) then the general multiplier will be divided by 0.8 to provide a higher multiplier. This practice is followed here using information on social classes I and II published by the Registrar General and derived from census data.[9] In addition adjustments are made, following Lydall and Tipping [7], to compensate for errors in occupational statements and for the unoccupied.[10]

It is interesting to note that Polanyi and Wood feel that "estimates . . . are highly sensitive to whichever assumption is made about the appropriate mortality rate" and that "there is scope for considerable error in estimating wealth . . . if the correction [for social class] is wrong, or wrongly applied" ([9], p.25). As with many of the points they raise however, Polanyi and Wood make no assessment of the quantitative importance to the estimates of the distribution of wealth. However, in the course of our research we have shown (see [4]) that the effect of variation in multipliers, while significant, is not large. Interestingly, the application of the social class differentials to higher estate classes results in a reduction in the estimated degree of concentration which is not perhaps what Polanyi and Wood had in mind.

---

9. For years where information is published on estates below the exemption level, these estates are multiplied by the general mortality multiplier.

10. The Inland Revenue also makes these adjustments; a fuller account of them is given in [5].

IV. The Distribution of Wealth In Scotland

We have now completed our discussion of the estate duty method and the extent to which we are able to compensate for its deficiencies. Next we report the application of this method to the published data on estates for Scotland in order to assess the degree of wealth concentration in Scotland and to examine how this compares with figures for England and Wales derived using the same method. This is, to our knowledge, the first time estimates of the distribution of wealth in Scotland have been produced although Wright [11] has earlier made an evaluation of the validity of Scottish thriftiness. This was done by analysing the size and composition of wealth-holdings in Scotland estimated by the Inland Revenue from estate data. He did not, however, include consideration of the distribution by size which is the subject of this paper.

In table 1 we present the full list of results of applying the technique outlined in section III to Scottish estate data for the years 1938 to 1969. Perhaps the most significant feature of this table is the constancy of the share of wealth held by the top 10 per cent in Scotland over the period since 1950 compared with a decline in the shares of the other groups considered. However, before this or any other features of the table are discussed in detail we must draw attention to certain aspects of the analysis which suggest that considerable caution should be adopted. These are essentially the problems which relate to Scotland in particular rather than to the general use of the estate duty method, and which are therefore discussed here rather than in the previous section.

The first of these is in some sense analogous to one of the examples of wealth missing from the estate duty statistics: that owned by British nationals domiciled abroad. In the case of Scotland the question of domicile assumes a greater significance since, as the Inland Revenue notes, for estate duty purposes "the division between England and Wales, and Scotland is according to where the estate is dealt with which depends broadly upon the domicile of the deceased and not upon where property is situated" ([6], p.174). Thus it must be recognised that we are concerned here strictly speaking with the distribution of wealth owned by Scots, not the distribution of wealth physically situated in Scotland. More important still is the possibility that a Scottish person's estate may not be dealt with in Scotland, so that it will not then appear in the statistics of Scottish estates.[11]

---

11. The Scottish Estate Duty Office feels however that this does not occur with any frequency.

Table 1   Distribution of Personal Wealth in Scotland, 1938-69

	Percentage of wealth owned by top				
	0.1%	1.0%	5.0%	10.0%	20.0%
1938	26.7	55.8	80.7	90.7	95.1
1950	17.0	42.5	68.9	78.7	84.6
1951	16.5	42.2	70.3	80.2	85.7
1952	17.0	39.6	65.4	75.9	82.4
1953	14.1	39.7	67.9	78.5	84.4
1954	15.3	41.5	69.5	79.3	85.1
1955	11.5	35.1	62.6	74.3	81.2
1956	12.1	35.7	64.4	73.3	80.5
1957	13.8	35.8	64.4	74.0	81.0
1958	12.2	35.5	64.4	74.1	81.1
1959	20.1	43.0	67.6	77.2	83.5
1960	10.2	37.6	66.5	78.7	87.9
1961	11.1	37.4	64.5	77.8	89.3
1962	14.2	40.4	67.8	81.7	90.9
1963	Not Available				
1964	12.0	37.2	66.5	79.4	90.2
1965	12.1	36.6	65.7	79.1	90.4
1966	11.9	35.8	64.4	78.4	90.0
1967	9.8	33.1	62.3	76.9	89.4
1968	10.8	33.4	63.6	78.7	90.0
1969	10.2	32.0	61.3	79.1	91.4

Notes

1. Since the estate duty method only provides estimates of points on a Lorenz curve the various percentage shares were derived using a log-linear interpolation routine.

2. The figures for the top 20 per cent are to be treated with considerable caution. They are greatly influenced by the interpolation routine used and are subject to a margin of possible error.

3. Clearly the figures for 1959 reflect unrepresentative sampling of deaths. This is dealt with more fully in the text, and the figures are excluded from further analysis.

Unfortunately there is nothing we can say *a priori* about the likely effects this will have on the estimated distribution of wealth. Perhaps the best we can do is express the hope that the trends over time are not influenced, although a comparison for a particular year with estimates for England and Wales may well be influenced by this factor.

The second problem peculiar to Scottish estate data is that a far higher proportion of estates dealt with in Scotland are recorded as "age not stated" than is the case in England and Wales.[12] For example in 1961-62 3 per cent of all estates were thus recorded in Scotland compared with less than 1 per cent in England and Wales. The usual procedure is to apply a weighted average of the multipliers for age-groups aged over 45 to the age not stated group, but there are no strong grounds for doing so and the outcome, in the case of Scotland, may be a bias in the final estimates.

The third, and probably the most important, consideration to be borne in mind when analysing table 1 concerns the representativeness of Scottish estate duty statistics as a sample of wealth-holdings in Scotland. Clearly problems of this nature are not absent from use of British estates as a whole, but for Scotland alone the possibility that the sample is not representative is far greater. This is because when estates are classified by the age and sex of the deceased and then by size of estate there are often very small numbers in some cells.[13] As we noted the size of certain cells is a problem for estimation of British wealth also and the Inland Revenue, when deriving the official estimates, combines observations across age-groups and applies a smoothing procedure. However the rationale for these adjustments is not at all obvious and we therefore do not adopt them in our work. Instead we attempt to compensate for an unrepresentative observation[14] by taking three year averages of the estimates and table 2 shows these for Scotland calculated from table 1, alongside equivalent figures for England and Wales.

The first point to note is that it is still the case that the share of the top 10 per cent of the adult population[15] remains almost constant between 1950-52 and 1967-69, dipping slightly in the late 1950s and then rising to over 78 per cent again. This trend is made more significant by the contrasting behaviour of the share of the top 10 per cent in England and Wales which shows a marked decline throughout the period, thus diverging from the Scottish figures after 1958. Conversely the shares of the top 0.1 per cent and 1.0 per cent in Scotland, and to a lesser extent that of the top 5 per cent, follow a

---

12. The Scottish Estate Duty Office could not explain why this was.

13. For example in Scotland in 1959-60, only 10 males died leaving an estate of over £250,000, and none was aged under 45.

14. The extraordinarily high share of the top 0.1 per cent in 1959 clearly provides an example of this.

15. All persons aged 25 or over.

Table 2   Distribution of Personal Wealth in Scotland and England and Wales, 1938-69

| | Scotland | | | | England and Wales | | | |
| | Percentage of wealth owned by top | | | | Percentage of wealth owned by top | | | |
	0.1%	1.0%	5.0%	10.0%	0.1%	1.0%	5.0%	10.0%
1938	26.7	55.8	80.7	90.7	26.6	54.2	76.8	85.7
1950–52	16.8	41.4	68.2	78.3	18.4	41.5	67.5	79.6
1953–55	13.6	38.8	66.7	77.4	16.7	41.1	66.4	77.0
1956–58	12.7	35.7	64.4	73.8	17.6	40.8	66.2	75.3
1960–62	11.9	38.5	66.3	79.4	14.0	35.3	60.6	73.1
1964–66	12.0	36.5	65.5	78.9	11.6	31.8	56.6	70.1
1967–69	10.3	32.8	62.4	78.2	11.6	31.2	55.6	68.4

Notes

1. The estimates for 1938 are as in table 1 since they are the only pre-war figures.

2. The estimates for 1959 were not used since they appeared to be unrepresentative.

trend much closer to that of England and Wales. In consequence it appears that in Scotland, unlike England and Wales,the redistribution of wealth that has occurred between 1950 and 1969 has been within the top 10 per cent of wealth-holders (300,000 individuals in 1969) rather than to groups lower down the distribution. For example while the share of the top 1 per cent has fallen from 41 per cent to 33 per cent, that of the next 4 per cent (i.e. 1 per cent-5 per cent) has risen slightly and that of the next 5 per cent (6 per cent-10 per cent) has risen markedly - from 20 per cent to 26 per cent.

A further point of interest is the extreme concentration of wealth which persists both in Scotland, and, to a lesser extent in England and Wales. This is perhaps best illustrated by noting that in table 2 we neglect to mention 90 per cent of the adult population. This group in 1967-69 owned just 22 per cent of total personal wealth in Scotland according to our estimates while in England and Wales it accounted for a little under a third. Nevertheless comparing this situation with 1938, the first year for which figures are available, suggests that this same group has doubled its share in both Scotland and England and Wales, so that some improvement is apparent. The extreme concentration in Scotland is however further underlined by examining the wealthiest group of all - the top 0.1 per cent.[16] In 1967-69 this group of approximately 3,000 individuals owned over 10 per cent of total wealth, about £640 million, implying an average figure of over £210,000.

Table 3   Distribution of Personal Wealth in Scotland, Northern Ireland, Republic of Ireland and England and Wales, 1966

	Percentage of wealth owned by top			
	0.1%	1.0%	5.0%	10.0%
Scotland (1965-67)	11.3	35.2	64.1	78.1
Northern Ireland (1966)	7.2	25.0	47.7	61.0
Republic of Ireland (1966)	10.4	33.6	62.9	74.1
England and Wales (1965-67)	11.1	31.0	55.7	69.4

Note

The estimates for Northern Ireland and the Republic of Ireland are log-linear interpolations of figures given in Lyons ([8], table 3, p.190).

16. It must be noted that it is at this level that problems of representativeness are likely to be most acute.

It is also of interest to compare the Scottish figures we have estimated with those for Ireland calculated by Lyons [8]. For the relevant year this is shown in table 3. Any conclusions must be guarded, since in many important ways we are not comparing like with like. However the comparison is interesting, in that the relative sizes of the populations of Ireland and Scotland are less diverse than those of England and Wales.

One important difference between the methods of estimation is that Lyons makes no allowance for the wealth of the excluded population,[17] assuming it to be equal to zero. This is clearly rather extreme, so that his figures are likely to suggest an unduly high degree of inequality. In spite of this we see that table 3 suggests a higher degree of wealth concentration in Scotland than in either the Republic of Ireland or Northern Ireland. Indeed compared with the latter country England and Wales also appear slightly more unequal. However we would strongly warn against placing any great emphasis on these apparent differences since as we have said the estimates are for many reasons not strictly comparable.

V. Some Tentative Suggestions

In this section we offer an assessment of the degree of inequality in Scotland in the context of the stated aim of the wealth tax, and present a number of very tentative suggestions to "explain" the divergences between Scotland and England and Wales seen in table 2.

There seems little doubt that distribution of wealth in Scotland is extremely unequal. Our results also suggest that the trend over time is at best only moving slowly in the direction of greater equality. Thus those who argue that there are already powerful forces causing the wealth distribution to become more equal are not supported, and their conclusion that a wealth tax is unnecessary cannot be justified.[18]

On the second question of why the degree of concentration appears so high in Scotland and why redistribution has been even less significant than in England and Wales, there are a number of

17. A further complicating factor is introduced by the fact that Lyons' "adult" population is aged 20 or over, whereas we have taken those aged 25 or over.

18. It is a further question, and one which we do not consider here, whether the particular wealth tax proposals made in the Green Paper [12] will achieve a substantial redistribution.

possibilities, none of which can alone supply the complete explanation. Perhaps the most likely, and certainly the most painless for those concerned about greater equality in Scotland, is that the figures based as they are on certain "statistical devices" fail to take account of factors which would otherwise indicate a state of affairs similar to that in England and Wales. We will briefly investigate this since it has clear implications for alternative explanations.

There are of course various ways in which our technique may be lacking and we look at two possibilities. First, it is important to note that over time the number of deaths recorded for estate duty purposes in Scotland, which form the basis of our estimates, is a declining proportion of the total for Britain. This means that when mortality multipliers are applied the excluded population in Scotland forms an increasing proportion of the British excluded population. These are the people about whom we probably know least, so that we cannot say categorically that the extreme inequality of the wealth distribution in Scotland is responsible for this phenomenon. If it is the converse, we need to explain the phenomenon for only then will we be sure that what we observe is not just a statistical quirk.

The second point is related to this. In our paper we attribute a certain average wealth to the excluded population. It is difficult to select the appropriate figure to use for this purpose. We have used figures which were originally applied to estimates for Britain but there are grounds for believing that the Scottish figure should be greater. For example Wright [11] notes the importance of traditional forms of wealth-holding in Scotland (deposit accounts, savings banks etc.) and this is particularly true of small wealth-holders. However to investigate this matter more fully requires more detailed knowledge of what sizes of estates are under-represented relative to England and Wales and of the asset composition of Scottish wealth both included in and excluded from estate duty statistics. This is not possible in the space available so that all we can say is that if our intuition is correct the estimates in this paper are an over-statement of the actual situation.

Finally we suggest an alternative explanation for the differences in table 2. Wright notes that, traditionally at least, home-ownership in Scotland has been the "exception rather than the rule" ([11], p.26). Thus since "part of the more rapid growth of wealth . . . has come from substantial investment in housing" it may be that regional variations in home-ownership are responsible, at least in part, for the observed differences. Support for this possible explanation comes from the published figures of the proportion of housing which is owner-occupied. In 1961, when the distribution of wealth in Scotland was fairly close to that in England and Wales, 25 per cent of the Scottish housing stock was owner-occupied compared to a British figure of 43 per cent. Ten years later, the distribution of wealth in Scotland had changed by less than that of England and Wales and home ownership was still relatively low. By 1971 for example owner-occupied houses in Scotland still represented only 29 per cent of the housing stock, whereas for Great Britain the figure had risen to 50 per cent, and in consequence Scotland still lagged substantially behind the rest of Britain in this respect. More recently however there is some indication that owner-occupation in Scotland may be accelerating.[19] If this trend continues, and if our suggestion has any validity, the wealth distribution in Scotland can be expected to move closer to that in the rest of Britain. On the other hand if we regarded council house property rights as wealth, the differences in table 2 may well be less pronounced because of the high proportion of local authority housing in Scotland, illustrating once again the importance of our choice of the definition of wealth.

VI. Summary

The distribution of wealth in Scotland, estimated from estate duty returns filed in Scotland, is extremely unequal. There is also no strong trend towards greater equality over time so that the proposed wealth tax is not a redundant piece of egalitarian machinery. Having said this much however, we must also remember that the figures on which the estimates are based and the technique used to derive the estimates have severe limitations. This means that we should treat our results with some caution and also express some reservations about the validity of the apparent differences between wealth in Scotland and that in England and Wales. One major problem associated with our estimates is the choice of the appropriate definition of wealth and it is clear that for at least one asset, housing, our choice may be critical. As the composition of Scotland's housing stock comes to resemble that of England and Wales we may be able to draw firmer conclusions on the basis of the methods of estimation we have applied.

---

19. By 1973 the figure for Scotland had increased to 32 per cent, so that the period 1971-73 saw a rise almost as great as that over the previous ten years.

References

[1]   Atkinson, A.B., "The Distribution of Wealth in Britain in the 1960s - the Estate Duty Method Re-Examined", in Smith, J. (ed.), *Personal Distribution of Income and Wealth,* National Bureau of Economic Research, 1974.

[2]   Atkinson, A.B., "Trends in the Distribution of Wealth - Theories and Evidence", paper presented to a Royal Economic Society conference on the *Personal Distribution of Incomes and Property* at Lancaster University in July 1974.

[3]   Atkinson, A.B., and Harrison, A.J., "Wealth Distribution and Investment Income in Britain", *Review of Income and Wealth,* 20, 2, June 1974, pp.125-142.

[4]   Atkinson, A.B., and Harrison, A.J., "Mortality Multipliers and the Estate Duty Method", mimeo.

[5]   Atkinson, A.B., and Harrison, A.J., *The Distribution of Personal Wealth in Britain,* Cambridge University Press, forthcoming.

[6]   Inland Revenue, *Inland Revenue Statistics 1974,* HMSO, 1974.

[7]   Lydall, H.F., and Tipping, D.G., "The Distribution of Personal Wealth in Britain", *Bulletin of the Oxford University Institute of Economics and Statistics,* 23, 2, February 1961, pp. 83-104.

[8]   Lyons, P.M., "The Size Distribution of Personal Wealth in the Republic of Ireland", *Review of Income and Wealth,* 20, 2, June 1974, pp.181-202.

[9]   Polanyi, G., and Wood, J.B., *How Much Inequality?,* Institute of Economic Affairs, 1974.

[10] Revell, J.R.S., *The Wealth of the Nation,* Cambridge University Press, 1967.

[11] Wright, L.C., "Personal Wealth in Scotland and Great Britain", *Three Banks Review,* 179, September 1968, pp.18-27.

[12] ———, *Wealth Tax,* Cmnd. 5704, HMSO, 1974.

Typeset, printed and bound in the University of Strathclyde

6/75/500/R141